TAROT FOR BEGINNERS

A Beginners Guide to Learning the Meaning and Secrets of Tarot Cards

(A Guide to Tarot Card Meanings and Tarot Reading)

Murray Landrum

Published by Sharon Lohan

© **Murray Landrum**

All Rights Reserved

Tarot for Beginners: A Beginners Guide to Learning the Meaning and Secrets of Tarot Cards (A Guide to Tarot Card Meanings and Tarot Reading)

ISBN 978-1-990334-66-5

All rights reserved. No part of this guide may be reproduced in any form without permission in writing from the publisher except in the case of brief quotations embodied in critical articles or reviews.

Legal & Disclaimer

The information contained in this book is not designed to replace or take the place of any form of medicine or professional medical advice. The information in this book has been provided for educational and entertainment purposes only.

The information contained in this book has been compiled from sources deemed reliable, and it is accurate to the best of the Author's knowledge; however, the Author cannot guarantee its accuracy and validity and cannot be held liable for any errors or omissions. Changes are periodically made to this book. You must consult your doctor or get professional medical advice before using any of the suggested remedies, techniques, or information in this book.

Upon using the information contained in this book, you agree to hold harmless the Author from and against any damages, costs, and expenses, including any legal fees potentially resulting from the application of any of the information provided by this guide. This disclaimer applies to any damages or injury caused by the use and application, whether directly or indirectly, of any advice or information presented, whether for breach of contract, tort, negligence, personal injury, criminal intent, or under any other cause of action.

You agree to accept all risks of using the information presented inside this book. You need to consult a professional medical practitioner in order to ensure you are both able and healthy enough to participate in this program.

Table of Contents

INTRODUCTION 1

CHAPTER 1: TAROT: WHAT IT IS AND ITS ORIGIN 3

CHAPTER 2: MODERN TAROT CARDS 15

CHAPTER 3: WHAT YOU NEED TO START TAROT READING. 27

CHAPTER 4: GOING DEEP WITH THE MAJOR ARCANA: FROM JUSTICE TO THE WORLD 39

CHAPTER 5: THE MAIN ENTITIES OF A TAROT DECK 59

CHAPTER 6: SPREADS OR HOW TO POSITION THE CARDS FOR A MORE REALISTIC READING 74

CHAPTER 7: COMPLETE COMPREHENSION OF THE MINOR ARCANA 80

CHAPTER 8: AMATEUR TAROT CARD READINGS 87

CHAPTER 9: SUIT OF WANDS 111

CHAPTER 10: SWORDS 117

CHAPTER 11: WHAT YOU NEED TO KNOW ABOUT SHUFFLING TAROT CARDS 121

CHAPTER 12: WHY PSYCHICS USE TAROT CARDS 126

CHAPTER 13: TIPS 132

CHAPTER 14: WHY DO YOU WANT TO LEARN HOW TO READ TAROT CARDS? 135

CHAPTER 15: SECOND SEPTENARY: ARCANA 7 TO 12 ANDROGONY 142

CONCLUSION.. 158

Introduction

This book has comprehensive information about reading Tarot Cards for beginners.

Learning to read Tarot cards is both, exciting and fun. As a beginner, you might find it a little challenging, but with time and practice, you will certainly start enjoying the reading more and will become better at it as well.

The Tarot comprises of 78 cards, each having its own special meaning. The cards need to be read in context, as one card tends to have different interpretations according to its location pertinent to other Tarot cards, its position in a spread as well as the question that is being asked. This means that with the 78 cards, countless card layouts (known as spreads) and myriads of decks, covering the Tarot card reading comprehensively won't be possible with just one book. This is why this book focuses mainly on the Major Arcana cards.

This guide will help you get insight into what tarot is, how it came into being, the uses of tarot cards, reading the Major Arcana cards and interpreting their meaning, and combining different cards. It will teach you the steps you need to take to read Tarot cards.

Thanks again for purchasing this book, I hope you enjoy it!

Chapter 1: Tarot: What It Is And Its Origin

The Tarot originated from northern Italy during the 15th century, where it was used as a card game similar to the modern game of Bridge. It started to be used in divinatory in Europe from 18th century.

The Tarot has 78 cards, with each card having its own unique meaning; these meanings are referred to as Tarot card meanings. The 78 cards are classified into 2 groups of cards, referred to as Arcana; one group has 22 cards and is known as Major Arcana while the other has 56 cards and is known as Minor arcana. The Major Arcana has 22 cards as shown below:

On the other hand, the Minor Arcana has 56 suit cards with four suits like the normal cards, the difference being instead of diamonds, spades, hearts, and clubs you have Pentacles, Wands, Cups, and Swords. The cards in these suits are numbered from 1-10 and they include- the king, queen, page and knight. The Minor Arcana usually represents small daily challenges in life.

Tarot cards have both an upright meaning and a reversed card meaning. You should know that Tarot readings require many years' experience. They need a deep understanding and knowledge of the Tarot because different readers tend to interpret the Tarot cards in their unique way.

The symbolism of the Tarot can provide different insights into the feelings and events in your life. It provides you with guidance when you need to make a decision; not answers actually but a different perspective on your situation. Therefore, the art of Tarot divination can be described as a way of using your intuition to gain a better understanding of your life, feelings, and emotions and those of others who are important to you.

How To Conduct A Tarot Reading

In this chapter, we will give you an insight on how to read Tarot. The first thing is definitely having a tarot deck. If you are a beginner, it is advisable to start with Rider Waite deck, which is very popular in the US. It is usually advisable to store your cards in a container in order to contain their energies and protect them. Also, since tarot cards pick the energy of those who use them, it is recommended to have your own cards that you alone use.

Here are steps to follow to do a tarot reading:

1. Create a Relaxing Atmosphere

This is important to both you and your guest in case you are helping other people read the Tarot. You will need to establish a sense of mutual respect with your guest or the questioner and then you can gather thoughts on the symbolism of the Tarot. Choose a peaceful and quiet atmosphere that does not have distraction. A right mindset is important when you are trying to get relaxed. This habit will help you create a focus for your thoughts. You can also place some items nearby that are special. It could be objects from nature like crystals, stones, shells, and plants.

If you want to, you can cover the floor or tablecloth you will be using to create a sort of uniform area. The cloth should be made of natural material like cotton, silk or wool. Also ensure that it is plain in color so that the images on the cards stand out from the background.

It is also important to always do the tarot reading the same place. This will build some kind of energy that will reinforce your practice.

2. Write a question

In most cases, you would want to do a tarot reading because you have a challenge or a problem. Something may be troubling you and you want a better understanding. So you will ask a question about your challenge and get an answer by reading the tarot cards. Before you can write the question, it is important to review the problem thoroughly. Think about the challenge, the situation and people involved as well as your options. Once you have successfully reviewed your situation, follow the following guidelines to write your question.

Accept that you have a role to play: Your tarot question should show that you have responsibility. This means that you cannot ask questions beginning with should or yes or no answers rather your questions should start like:

How can I improve…?

Can you give me some insight into…?

What is the purpose or lesson of…?

And such

Keep options open: Don't come to tarot reading with a made up mind when you want the help with tarot reading. It is essential to keep your options open. Instead of asking, "How do I break up with my boyfriend" you can instead ask, "How do I get along with my boyfriend?"

Only provide necessary details: You don't want your question to be too narrow or just too vague.

Be positive and neutral

3. Ask your question

Remove your cards from where you put them and hold them in your hands then place the other hand on top of them. You can then make an opening statement if you want to. Once you have done that, you can ask your question either by reading it or from memory.

4. Shuffle the cards

Shuffle the cards however you want to and as you do so, concentrate on your question. Your goal should be to focus on overall intent instead of details.

5. Cut the cards

Once you think you have shuffled enough, stop then put the cards in front of your face down ensuring that the short edge is closest to you then do the following:

Get a number of cards from the pile in front of you and put this pile to your left.

Get another set of cards and put this further to your left

Regroup the cards in whatever way you want. Don't think too much about it, just do it.

6. Decide the spread you will use

Tarot card spread simply refers to how you will lay out the cards physically on the table in order to interpret after shuffling the cards. The thing with spreads is that there are different kinds of spreads. However, we will provide a few examples that you can get started with. As you look at the spreads, you will notice that they are organized from 1 through to a certain number. This simply refers to the order that you deal the cards after shuffling and cutting.

Celtic cross spread

This is one of the most popular spread used. Owing to its popularity, there are many variations to its layout. Below is a common layout that you can use.

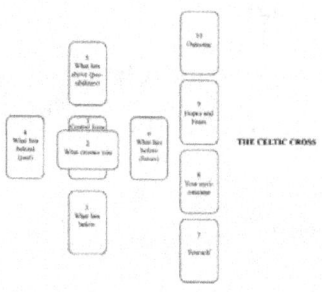

Horseshoe spread

This spread is a variation of the celtic cross spread and is effective for thorough analysis of a particular situation or question.

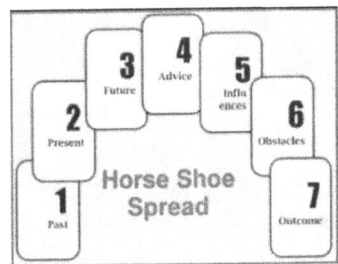

Tree of life spread

This spread looks at all the major factors affecting your present situation.

Source: Psychic Library

1. Ideals
2. Creativity

3. Wisdom

4. Virtues

5. Being force

6. Beauty and health

7. Lust, lovers and instincts

8. You as a creator

9. Psychic self

10. Physical self

Three Card Spread

This is one of the simplest spreads and is most suitable if you are a beginner.

Source: Glauxnet

Romany Spread

With this spread, you deal 21 cards and arrange them in three rows as show below. The top most row indicates the past, the center one indicates the present and the bottom on signifies the future. You may also do a reading according to the columns and have 7 columns. Let us have a look at this closely.

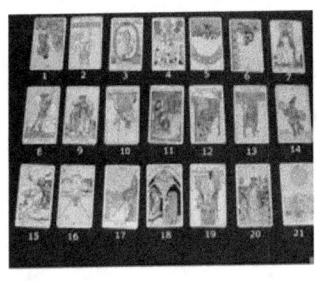

Column 1: Self

Column 2: Personal environment

Column 3: Hopes and dreams

Column 4: Known factors

Column 5: Hidden destiny

Column 6: Short-term future

Column 7: Long-term outcome

We may not cover all spreads here, so for more spreads, you can check here.

In the following chapter, we will look closely at tarot card meanings and interpretations.

Chapter 2: Modern Tarot Cards

While it started way back during the Renaissance Period, tarot cards are still popular today for their remarkable insights on the different periods throughout centuries.

Originally used as playing cards, the tarot garnered more following among those who are interested in the occult practice especially among mystics in the 1800s.

Today, more people rely on modern tarot and oracle cards that are less traditional in their structure for divine guidance to light forecast of what's coming in the future.

While standard decks are still appealing, like Raider Waite Collections and Doreen Virtue's Mystical Packs, new modern crops are starting to draw interest to modern mystics.

The tarot deck

To completely understand how a Tarot Deck works, you have to familiarize yourself with the composition of the deck. Each deck is made up of 78 cards divided into three major categories.

The first twenty-two cards of the Tarot Deck comprise the Major Arcana, and the Minor Arcana accounts for 56 minor cards following the Major cards.

Each card holds a particular symbolism and meaning. In the card reading, the effect of each card varies, based on the following factors:

Which kind of spread (e.g., success, relationship, Celtic cross, and three-card spreads)

The placement of cards

The connection of the cards with each other

The deck type of deck used by the reader (e.g., "The Deviant Moon," "The New Mythic," and "The Rider-Waite-Smith")

Whether a particular card is in upright or reversed positions

When there is much emphasis placed on Major cards, the Minor cards support role to the Tarot deck is relatively significant. Therefore, to familiarize yourself with the Tarot Deck, it is crucial to understand the function of all cards and not just one section of the deck.

Types of Tarot Decks

Frankly, there are tons of different varieties of tarot decks and there is no official tarot deck used anywhere. A lot of them are similar, but there are those that have a lot of striking differences in theme and imagery. With that said, we are only going to list down the top most famous and essential tarot decks.

Aleister Crowley Thoth Tarot

This deck has fantastic artwork and is also considered as a classic tarot deck. Thoth Tarot deck contains 80 cards with three different versions of the card Magus. Also known as Crowley Thoth Tarot and Toth Tarot. A beautiful and classic deck indeed, but it is one of the darkest and most controversial card deck.

Shadowscapes Tarot

This tarot deck is a must for all those fantasy lovers out there. Each card is endowed with stunning images and the watercolors added more to the mythical sight. Shadowscape follows the Rider-Waite theme, it even comes with a book.

The designs are inspired by folklore, fantasy and nature. Fans and enthusiasts waited six long years before this tarot card deck made its debut. The most noticeable and appreciated in this tarot deck's design is the fact that everything is painted in a way that gives it the illusion of fluid motion. Hands down to the artists

Stephanie Pui-Mun Law on her card designs.

Deviant Moon Tarot

What makes Deviant Moon Tarot is its design. Each card is surreal, unique and sometimes quite disturbing. A borderless edition is available and a white booklet comes with the deck. You see, the theme is all about cemeteries and mental asylums, it kind of gives the users a sneak peek into the deepest and darkest part of their subconsciousness. Patrick Valenza, the creator, really put the dark and mystery into the twisted forms of nightmares and the elements of death. All the figures in the deck are nonhuman, the colors are gloomy and a lot of small details has something to do with the creator's childhood and imagination.

DruidCraft Tarot

From the name of the tarot deck itself, it's evident that the drawings are based on Druidry and nature spiritualties. Also, as you guessed, it has a lot of natural elements in it. Just by looking at the tarot deck, you might even see the movement of the characters alongside their calm background. Keep in mind that there is a little nudity involved in both male and female, but that doesn't mean that they look any less attractive. It's incredible to think how brilliant Stephanie Carr-Gomm, Philip Carr-Gomm and Will Worthington were when they created DruidCraft Tarot and another tarot deck called Druid Animal Oracle.

Legacy of the Divine Tarot

You can't go wrong with the name, everything about this deck is simply divine and amazing. Not only are the designs rich, but also the color and ideas. Don't be afraid to own this deck if you're not a tarot expert, because it won't matter. Looking at each magical scene, all the details really to pop up since each one has a highly realistic and digital design.

You really got to hand it to the artist, graphic designer and creator Ciro

Marchetti. Though he has minimal experience and background when it comes to tarot cards, he still managed to design a deck that didn't deviate too much from the original ideas.

Wild Unknown Tarot

A tarot deck that focused on nature, wild animals, symbolism and a lot of black and white. There are only a few splashes of color on each card, but that doesn't mean that it lacked beauty. If it was possible, the lack of color gave it even more charm. Each line in every card can speak for themselves.

This kind of theme and design is so unique that it would be a crime not to have in your collection, it's also one of the reasons why it's popular. The creator, Kim Krans, really put a lot of thought into each stroke and small details.

Victorian Romantic Tarot

This tarot deck is based on the engravings from the artists of the 19th century. Historical and the Victorian era are the main themes of this deck. When you look at the 78 cards on this tarot deck, you will be transported back in time. It's filled with everything concerning the Victorian passions and medieval styles.

The creators Alex Ukolov and Karen Mahony sought to put various women from different levels in society; from the queen to the poor. Not only that, but there are intricate images and engravings scattered all over the cards.

Gaian Tarot

Gaian Tarot is solely dedicated to the earth, nature and Gaia herself. Before, this deck was only available as majors-only set until the minors were completed. This tarot deck is very traditional, from the number of cards to most of the titles and more. All the designs are so down-to-earth, they show communities interacting with nature and with each other.

Not to mention tons of compilation of intricate designs and interpretative work. It's a fresh break from all the kings and queens of most of the tarot decks, better thank creator Joanna Powell Colbert for that.

Rider-Waite Tarot

This is a classic among all the classics in tarot decks, also the most famous. This widely circulated deck is also known as Rider Tarot, Waite Tarot and Waite-Smith Tarot. It doesn't matter if you're a beginner or an expert in tarot reading, this deck should be added to your collection. This deck is available in multiple formats like miniature, pocket, standard and giant. The cards in this deck may not have the most colorful and extravagant designs, but that doesn't make them any less enjoyable.

The minor Arcana-a short introduction

The Minor Arcana reveals mostly the stages of events and everyday happenings. These cards display ordinary people engaged in insignificant activities like sleeping, drinking, quarreling, dancing, and many more. Notice how human behaviors trigger these actions. They appear during gentle transitions that can be temporary and have minimal effects on the life of the individual.

The Minor Arcana Tarot Cards meanings signify events that naturally happen relative to the law of human nature.

Cards included in the Minor Arcana describe people, events, and situations that we encounter while we are going through our journey in life. They signify events that are within our control and indicate what we must do.

The Minor Arcana contains these Court Cards:

The Page

Knight

King

Queen

These cards serve as a bridge linking the Major and Minor Arcana by describing various archetypal personal types.

The Ace card indicates the beginning while number 10 marked the end. Similarly, the numbering of the court cards represents our understanding of situations in an individual reflecting either personality types or the actual person.

Tarot Journal

When you keep a Tarot journal, you will find yourself putting into words the fears and thoughts that you have without the worry of facing any criticism. This could be your own personal property, like your diary. There is a considerable benefit behind maintaining a tarot journal.

This is because you will be able to able to write your thoughts, insights, feelings and your observances. You can be whoever you want to be without having to think twice! You will find that the journal has become the central aspect of your life. This could be your story since you will be able to write whatever you choose to without having a fear of being judged. When you read the journal in the future, you will find yourself happier since you will be able to view your growth.

You could enter entries into your journal without any hesitation and at any time! You will also need to give yourself some time to write in your journal about your experiences with the tarot. When you have understood the value of the journal that you are keeping, you will find that it has become your best friend, which will work well when it comes to recording your feelings or your trauma, joys, gains, success, loss or grief.

You will need to record the date and the time of every Tarot reading that you do. You will need to maintain the record of the layout that you have used too. When you finish each reading, you will find yourself one step closer in your journey to achieve wisdom. When you have a good record of your Tarot reading, you will be able to observe yourself well and will also find yourself growing.

Chapter 3: What You Need To Start Tarot Reading.

There are a number of implements and objects that you can use when you're doing a reading. These may help you achieve the results you want:

Decks

So, the first thing you'll need is a deck. It's obviously a must when you're doing a reading. The things you should take into account when you're out shopping for one have been mentioned earlier, but let's make a little recap. Basically, you should evaluate the deck's imagery, find one that you feel you can understand completely; and then 'feel' the deck, see if it feels right or not when you're using it.

Spreads

Once you've gotten some cards of your own, you should also research spreads. These are the way you lay out the cards and the relationship between them. You might look into the topic and feel intimidated by some of the more complicated ones. If you can barely understand one card, never mind ten or more of them all together. So, when you're a true beginner you may not want to start off with complicated stuff, and it is quite alright.

You can always just draw one card. And then after a while, when your understanding of the cards has increased, look up some three-card spreads on the internet, you can use the one mentioned in the guide book you're using, or you might just want to do it intuitively. As you progress, don't feel the need to stick to the spreads you've found, and the spreads that other people have made. They are supposed to be a sort of training wheel system until you feel confident enough to make your very own.

Candles, incense, and essences

Once you have a deck and a spread you'll need a place that feels safe and right. Somewhere you feel sacred in your mind.

This feeling may be achieved by conditioning it to what you're going to do. Like smells. If you burn some candle and incense then you'll be more relaxed and might be more in-tune with the cards and what they say.

In general, aroma therapy is very common for the people belonging to this community. Essences can heal your moods and your physical aches, and hence, can make you feel more at home and safe in your sacred place. Normally, these tools like the candles can be found in the same place where you got your tarot cards. Not that finding natural essences is difficult but finding a deck might just be a little hard, so there you have a tip.

Crystals or gemstones

Another thing that might help with the tuning-into and with feeling safe and relaxed is using crystals. There is really nothing else to explain for this term. I really do mean minerals made in the earth, like Rose Quartz, Lapis Lazuli, and

Tiger's Eye. The chemical structure found in these minerals is said to invest them with a sort of memory, and that is what is used. People push their emotions and intentions into the crystal, and 'program' it. Once that is done, the crystal will remember it and radiate that emotion or intention into the environment. You'll see then how you could use crystals to make a room feel a certain way.

There are many other things that you can use to help you, but just remember that the idea is to help, not to be in the way. A person might find they can do a reading in their living room without doing anything else to it. They might like to smell some coconut while they do it, or they might want to feel lots of love while at it. Or they might want to have everything going on at the same time.

For different people, there are different things that work and hinder them. The most important thing to decide on what works and what doesn't is to trust your intuition, which is a skill you'll need in almost everything regarding this topic.

Tools that get in the way

People work differently, so this section is a little more personal. Some might feel that wearing tinkling jewelry hinders a reading. Some may feel that the sound is calming and helps. Here are some things that most would agree get in the way:

Caffeine

If you come from a normal type of background you'll find that the things you eat and drink, affects your performance quite a lot. When you practice yoga, for example, if you ate too much just a little while before the session, you might not be able to do some positions or reach the same places you normally could. When you do a reading, your mind needs to be blank and in peace. If coffee makes it hard for you to sit still, or makes you feel fuzzy, jittery, and on edge, you might want to avoid it while doing a reading. However, if you're the type of person that feels nothing after drinking coffee, then that is alright too. Just go with what feels right.

Alcohol

One glass is just fine, maybe even two if alcohol doesn't affect you much. But becoming intoxicated is not something that would help during a reading. Not only because being drunk wrecks your concentration skills and thought process, but also because of the image you have created for yourself. If you are a professional worker and are drunk during the working hours, then potential clients, who might already be prejudiced against tarot readers won't take you seriously. In any kind of job, being intoxicated is a big no, why should it be any different just because you're your own boss?

The other thing to take into account is that tarot cards are quite serious business, as is the information provided by them. Think about the intentions I mentioned before. What if due to the state you're in, you end up doing a reading with bad intentions? What if you say something wrong, or word it in the wrong way? As a tarot reader, you should always remember that you're dealing with other people's lives, and you can change them completely with just one word.

Drugs

Yes, everybody knows the majority of them are not legal, but people continue to be found using them. That is not what we're here to discuss, though. Like with alcohol, drugs hinder your concentration and many other areas of your brain and mind. That is the reason why you shouldn't partake into those activities while doing a reading. If you read tarot cards for a living or if you're doing it for a friend, think about the way people will see you and think about the way your intentions and wording might affect their lives.

As an added note, there are things clients or friends can do to hinder a reading too.

The major ones are also drugs and alcohol because it will be hard to make a reading if the person is not really present if they are not really pay attention.

Think about it this way: the clients ask the question, and in order to do that they should focus. But being intoxicated in any way will shatter their ability to focus. Plus, there is quite a high possibility that the person doesn't remember the information you're giving them. In that case, what good is it? If it's a client, reschedule for another time. Turn them down, you might lose money, but it'll be for their own good. If it's a friend, do the same thing, turn them down.

Where to find your necessities

There are many places that you can go to when looking for any of the aforementioned tools. In this era of technology, the first place I'd recommend would be the internet. Keep in mind, however, that doing your shopping this way can be quite difficult. If you'll notice, most of the advice on how to choose your essences, your crystals or your deck is based around 'what feels right'. Touching what you're buying and analyzing your body's reaction to it is almost a must. Through the internet, you are sort of bypassing it. You'll need to step up your intuition to make the right choices.

The second recommendation would be the internet too. But in this case as a means of finding physical shops that are nearby. You're looking for a mystic or an occult shop, or a metaphysical bookstore. That kind of thing. Normally, where they do tarot readings, you'll find the things you're looking for. Or you can do your shopping in separate places. Candles, essences, and incense can be found in head shops. And you can find tarot decks in some bookstores.

Spreads

You might've been thinking, spreads were among the necessities mentioned above, and they can be. If you find a store specializing in tarot and other mystic things, you might want to ask for some guidebooks. If not, you can ask in bookstores to see if they have anything. These books will give you card interpretation tips and some of the more popular (and sometimes basic) spreads. However, finding spreads is far easier than finding the other things you'll need. In this case, the internet is great help. You can find some guidebooks online and download them or read them for free. Also, there are lots of tarot sites and most offer some spreads for free.

Remember, though, that spreads are not something you should be dependent on. The idea is that you understand the way cards relate to each other in a spread and then make your own. To do this, you'll just have to name the relationship between cards and the particular area the card drawn should provide insight of.

For example, let's suppose you make a boyfriend spread that in the end should give you pertinent information on the guy you're dating or thinking of dating. The first card is the way you feel about the guy, the second is the person you're considering, the third is something to consider before dating him or stepping up the relationship, the fourth is the weak point between you two, and the fifth is a final note, an overall card that relates to all the others already drawn. Like that, you can make your very own spread for just about anything.

Important

Yes, all these tools are supposed to help you. But that is the only thing they should do. Helping is not the same as supporting. The word "helping" implies that you put in your own effort as well. So, beware of getting attached to things and using them as crutches. If you begin to feel that you simply cannot do a reading without a blue candle in the room, or if you require a Quartz stone to be able to read the tarot cards, then alarm bells should be ringing everywhere in your mind. This type of feeling and behavior is not alright at all. It is exactly what turns a good thing into a bad thing.

When you read tarot cards, you use your sixth sense, your 'intuition', quite a lot, and when you're starting out, candles and crystals can help enhance that sense. As you become more skillful and adept at doing readings, your sixth sense should develop, and the tools shouldn't be necessary. However, if used in excess, tools can blight your sixth sense, then the damage done will be far worse than the good they did. In general, you need only your cards and yourself, the rest is decoration.

Chapter 4: Going Deep With The Major Arcana: From Justice To The World

In this chapter, the discussion for the major arcana will continue. This time, the focus will be from Justice to The World cards.

What to expect from the remaining cards

From this point forward, you might notice some differences in the cards. This is because this half of the major arcana illustrates the challenges that can be experienced in the path towards understanding and fulfillment. There are even cards that may be quite alarming for people, such as Death and The Devil. However, by studying the meanings attributed with each card carefully, it will be easier to provide a better interpretation if ever these alarming cards are revealed in a reading.

Justice

This card commonly has the following positive associations:

Arbitration

Balance

Fairness

Integrity

Justice

Responsibility

Truth

However, the Justice card may also be associated with the following negative keywords:

Bad advice

Bad judgment

Bias

Injustice

Prejudice

If this card is included in a reading, it represents fairness and equality when it comes to dealing with others. This is a good sign for areas where such is important; this includes business deals and partnerships. This also signifies that a wrong committed to the client in the past will be corrected, or it could also mean that they are in search of justice for another person.

However, the card could also signify injustice. This simply means that the client might not get what is due for them; some situations include business deals that do not favor both parties, and not getting the expected legal decisions even if they think that they're right. It could also mean that they may get bad advice or receive bad judgment.

The Hanged Man

The following words are just some of the positive associations with this card:

Deliverance

Flexibility

Rebirth

Release

Transition

However, this card can also have the following negative associations:

Easily influenced

Inflated ego

Lack of willpower

Martyrdom

Materialism

This card is most often the symbol of self-sacrifice, and it pertains to either emotional or material self-sacrifice. This gives the individual an ability to adjust to different circumstances. The card also signifies a "pause" in the person's life, and that they should remain in this state until someone or something is sacrificed for greater gain. Another concept represented by this card would be anxiety, stress, and ill health, and somehow implies that the person should be patient until such has passed.

Unfortunately, The Hanged Man can also represent selfishness, as well as "looking like a martyr" so that they could have leverage over others. It can also be associated with a weak willpower, which could lead them in the wrong path and result in missing crucial opportunities.

Death

The appearance of the Death card in a reading could mean the following:

Clearance

Endings

Sweeping change

Transformation

Unfortunately, it could also have the following negative associations:

Fear of change

Loss of friendship

Loss of opportunity

Stagnation

While the name of the card itself is quite frightening, it does not actually tell that somebody will be dying. Rather, the card represents the unavoidable end and beginning of something. This card is a sign that shocking and unforeseen events will occur, and that this event will serve as the starting point of another. To simplify, Death signifies that the time for transformation will be coming soon.

For the negative association, Death tells of the possibility that the person might be afraid of the transforming event that they are about to experience. If the reverse position is shown in the spread, it simply implies that the person should be ready to show what they are capable of. Another negative association with the card – stagnation – also signifies the person's resistance to change even if it important that they do. This resistance could lead to missing out on crucial opportunities (thus, leading the person to be unchanged or "dead").

Temperance

Some of the positive keywords associated with this card are the following:

Compromise

Harmony

Health

Moderation

Peace

Self-control

On the other hand, it may also be associated with the following negative keywords:

Conflict

Domestic strife

Impatience

Lack of foresight

Quarrels

The Temperance card is closely attributed to self-control, which enables the person to handle unpredictable aspects and be able to bring positive results. It is also a sign that they will be experiencing a time of harmony in their relationships, which should be enjoyed. The card also emphasizes the importance of moderation and that spirituality could bring them comfort. Some people even say that the card is a representation of the angel or spirit who is watching over them.

However, the Temperance card could also mean that if a person lacks insight about a situation and is impatient when it comes to making a decision, it could cause conflicts and may even hinder their progress.

The Devil

The positive associations of this tarot card are as follows:

Commitment

Permanence

However, it can also have any of the following negative associations:

Anger

Entrapment

Greed

Ignorance

Lust

Obsession

Tyranny

Just like Death, the name of the card somehow gives a negative meaning. Fortunately, there are still positive concepts attributed to this card. This is because if The Devil is included in a person's reading and is revealed in an upright position, it could signify commitment to a relationship or even marriage (which is a form of permanence).

However, the card mostly warns people when it is in a reverse position. This is because the card signifies addiction, lust, and temptation – all of which does not provide a favorable outcome. This could serve as a warning, as The Devil may be representing obsessions or people that may not be good for the client. Therefore, it is imperative that they should carefully examine their situation. It also warns them of the possible grave consequences that may be experience if they let lust, greed, and power become their motivation. Having The Devil in a tarot card reading is a sign that they need to change their course of action before it becomes too late.

Taking the card as a warning sign, it can still be implied that The Devil is helpful despite the multiple negative keywords associated with it.

The Tower

This card has the following positive associations:

Blessing in disguise

Necessary change

Re-evaluation

However, The Tower can also have any of the following negative associations:

Disaster

Disruption

Downfall

Sudden change

Although the name of the card itself is not something to worry about (unlike Death and The Devil), the illustration of the card somehow provides its appearance in a spread with a negative meaning. While it could be difficult to find a positive meaning for this card, it could still tell the person that unexpected events will be experienced. These events, in turn, will provide them with an opportunity that could make the person wiser and stronger. It can also encourage the individual so that they will see these sudden events as a way to force a change that will bring them more benefit than harm.

However, The Tower can also represent misery or unnecessary pain. It could be that the client will be accused of something by mistake and suffer punishment that they shouldn't be experiencing.

But despite the apparent unpleasant meaning of this card, it should be remembered that this event shall pass. Once it does, they can either be taken to a new path or are presented with new opportunities.

The Star

Some of the positive associations with this card are the following:

Generosity

Good health

Hope

Serenity

Spiritual awareness

Wishes coming true

This card, though, may also have the following negative associations:

Lack of trust

Pessimism

Self-doubt

The Star can be considered as the opposite of The Tower, primarily because it is associated with many positive concepts. If this card is part of the spread, it signifies positive things such as hope and optimism, getting the client's faith renewed - even the possibility of receiving unexpected gifts (material or otherwise). It is also a good sign if they are thinking of starting an enterprise or getting in a relationship. The Star is also a sign that good times will be experienced in many aspects. This includes health-related issues, travel, and even endeavors that are educational or artistic in nature.

However, The Star could also warn the client of the dangers when there is too much negativity and self-doubt, which may cause them to lose good opportunities. But despite the pessimism, they will still be surprised with the great amount of luck that they're experiencing.

The Moon

This card is mostly associated with the following positive concepts:

Illumination

Imagination

Unexpected possibilities

It may also be associated with the following negative concepts:

Bewilderment

Confusion

Deceit

Fear

Highly charged emotions

Lies

When this card appears, it is a sign that the client will be experiencing situations that involve confusion and highly charged emotions. But despite the fear of the situation, they can be sure that they will be guided towards the right way and that everything will be fine in the end. It could also lead the client to artistic expression such as music, writing, or art. This, in turn, may give them unexpected opportunities.

On the other hand, this card can also signify the lack of progress mainly because of the client's fears or anxieties. It can also serve as a warning that they are being lied to or deceived – which may even be the cause of their anxiety.

The Sun

This card has the following positive associations:

Enlightenment

Fulfillment

Good health

Greatness

Happiness

Love

Vitality

However, The Sun can also have the following negative associations:

Delays

Inflated ego

Misjudgment

Potential failure

The appearance of The Sun in a spread mostly signifies joyous times. This includes holidays, news about conceiving a baby or the child being born soon, fun time for family and friends, and even pleasant relationships. Generally, The Sun assures the person with a happy ending and dismisses negativity.

However, the card can still have minimal negative associations. One such negative meaning would be the possibility of delays (either for achievements or the client's plans). It is also a warning for arrogance, which may be brought about by having an inflated ego.

Judgment

This card can have any of the following positive associations:

Absolution

New potential

Rebirth

Rejoicing

Rewards for past efforts

It can also have these negative associations:

Delays

Fears

Guilt

Loss

Obstinacy

Self-reproach

If this card is in an upright position, it is a sign that the client will be experiencing success as well as reap the rewards for their past efforts. It also represents the coming of an opportunity that should not be ignored once it does, as this decision or project could change their life significantly. If ill health is an issue, this card is also a sign that recovery will come.

However, the card can also be attributed to stubbornness. If the client continues to refuse in adapting change, it will only cause delays. It also warns the person of self-doubt as well as guilt of the mistakes committed in the past. The card may also be a sign that fear (of almost everything) will be experienced.

The World

Some of the positive attributions with this card are as follows:

Completion

Fulfillment

Joy

Satisfaction

Success

Wholeness

However, this card can also have these negative associations:

Delays

Impatience

Lack of will

Stagnation

The World card is a sign that whatever it is that the client desires will be coming to them. This is also a time for experiencing success and be recognized with what they have given. Its appearance in a spread also represents a time for holidays, enjoyment, travel, having time with their loved ones, having an opportunity to indulge in the material things that they desire, and being in a rewarding relationship. Generally, this card could also indicate the end of one stage and the beginning of another.

However, this card could also mean that some delays will be experienced, and that the client still has to overcome some difficulties before success comes. This is a sign that they should not give up, now that they're very close to achieving what they want.

Getting more practice in tarot card reading

Now that you know about the positive and negative meanings for each card in the major arcana, it's time to test your skills through practice. In order to further familiarize yourself with the meanings of each major arcana card, you need to simulate an actual reading.

Start by taking out all the major arcana cards from your deck and shuffling them. Ask a question that you would want answered, and pick three cards.

The 1st card is a reflection of your (or the client's) current situation. Recall the meanings attributed with the card and take note of whatever the card is telling you regarding your situation.

The 2nd card is the advice given for you. Think through as to what the card is suggesting you to do.

The 3rd card is the outcome card. What do you think will happen? Consider the meaning of the card and write it down in your journal.

Chapter 5: The Main Entities Of A Tarot Deck

A usual tarot cards deck has 78 cards. The 78 cards are divided into the major and the minor arcanas. This chapter focuses on the major arcana cards and their meanings. The word arcana mean 'Profound Secret'. According to the alchemists, the arcana tell us the secrets of nature. But it is a common belief that the Tarot cards are a collection of secrets about our universe.

The Major Arcana

There are 22 cards that form the major arcana of the tarot deck. These cards are the center of the deck. Each card symbolizes some aspect of any experience that you might have had in your life. These experiences could also be those that could happen in the future. These represent the influences that are inherent to human nature. Each of these cards has a name and a number. Some names directly give you the meaning of the card – Strength,

Justice and temperance. Other cards personalize the approach that we have towards life or to a situation – the Magician or the Hermit. There are multiple other cards that depict the astronomical bodies like the Sun, Stars and the Moon. These three cards represent the astronomical influence on our lives.

The cards from the major arcana are special. They bring out reaction from within us that are deep and complex. These cards are always given more importance during a reading. When one of these cards occurs in the reading you know that the situation at hand is not temporary. They represent the problem at hand and how you are feeling at the moment. They also tell you what you are worried about. The major arcana are a unit on their own. There are different schemes that have been developed through numerology, astrology and other esoteric sciences that help you understand the human condition in a situation. Divination is one of the most accurate ways of reading the Tarot.

Cards constituting the Major Arcana

There are 22 cards that fall under the major arcana. This section lists the names of these cards and how they can be interpreted for a reading.

The Fool

This card shows that you are spontaneous. It states that you face the world with your head held high. It marks beginnings and starting a new adventure. You are free spirited and take on the world bravely. You possess high trust and believe in commitment. You have high ideals and are capable of understanding the ways of this world and beginning something with a strong mind. However, you do not consider the problems that might occur because of such an attitude. You might take unnecessary risks and make foolish mistakes. Your risks might not always pay off positively owing to being irrational.

The Magician and the High Priestess

The magician is active and depicts your conscious awareness. It also states that you have a charm and the will power to take over any challenge that life throws at you. You are marked by power and skill and can showcase immense concentration power. You are resourceful and have the means to tackle anything that comes you way. However, you can be extremely manipulative and try and solicit work out of others. You may not always have a plan to follow and will prefer to dive nose deep into something without considering its aftermath.

The high priestess on the other hand depicts your mysterious unconscious. This card states that you have an inherent potential that you have not realized. It deals with high power and a strong sense of intuition. So you have the chance to reach the very heights of life and are capable of tapping into your inner conscious to seek answers. Once you realize this potential you will be able to achieve whatever you aim to achieve.

However, you might have a lot of hidden agendas and might not pay keen attention to what your inner voice has to say to you. This aspect needs to be sorted out.

The Empress

This card depicts everything that is natural and sensual in the world. It is also called Juno. Juno is the Roman goddess who is the Queen of all the Roman Gods. So it depicts fertility and femininity. It also depicts our beauty and natural attractiveness. It signifies an abundance that you have in terms of your good looks and your fertility. However, it also signifies your lack of creativity in anything that you do as also your tendency to not be independent and rely on others for everything.

The Emperor

This card depicts the Father. It will show that you are subjected to multiple rules in life. It also means that you will do wonders because of these very rules. It basically signifies a father figure and the authority that it brings along. You are extremely structured and have a very solid foundation. You are confident and deal with life in an authoritative manner. However, you can be extremely dominating and incapable of allowing others to have authority in your presence. You can be quite rigid and not be open to being met with flexibility.

The Hierophant

This card tells you that you are ready to be educated. It says that you will only be with a group of people whom you are able to connect to. You would not be comfortable about not meeting people who are new to you. It also signifies religion and leading a group through spiritual guidance. The hierophant pertains to conformity and traditional beliefs. But this makes the card old fashioned and brings along many restrictions. It constantly challenges the status quo and wished to bring in a positive change through religious and spiritual means.

Image Courtesy: Nocturbulous

The Lovers

This card can be interpreted as you being ready to enter into a relationship. But this does not necessarily mean that it will be a healthy relationship. You might have to work on the relationship to make it last. It signifies love and compassion and the bringing together of two people. It deals with the choice that the two have in terms of forging into a relationship. However, it will also signify disharmony and an imbalance in the love structure. There might also be a misalignment in the values of the lovers.

The Chariot

The Chariot depicts your will power. It shows that you can wield you will power in order to achieve greatness and victory in any given situation. It pertains to control and the will of a person. It also signifies victory and the determination that one has towards attaining life's goals. The person goes after his or her goals through calculated assertions. However, this might cause them to lose direction and end up exerting too much force in the wrong direction.

Strength, Judgment and Justice

These cards depict the names themselves. If these cards arise during a reading, it can be interpreted that you are a very strong person and that you take just measure. You take the moral high ground every time.

If you get the strength card then it signifies that you are strong and have a lot of courage. It also means that you have immense self-control and a great deal of compassion for others. But the negatives of this includes having a profound weakness and indulging in self-doubt. It also signifies a lack of self-control.

If you get the justice card then it signifies your love for the truth and a fair game. It adheres to the principles of cause and effect and what it takes to deliver justice to the righteous. However, it can also signify a lack of virtue and dishonesty. There is also a lack of accountability and you might try and take advantage of such a situation.

The judgment card signifies rebirth and an inner calling. The judgment card is meant to absolve sins. This means that the person is in a position to deliver justice through judgment. However, the person will indulge in self-doubt and refuse to understand and accept their own sins and mistakes. They will indulge in self-examination and look for negatives but not act on them.

Temperance

The temperance card signifies balance and patience. It also signifies purpose and meaning. However, it can also signify an imbalance and a lack of vision. There might be an excess of balance, which can sometimes be a bad thing.

Hermit

This card depicts that you are in search of knowledge. The knowledge here could be anything at all! As the name suggests, the hermit is determined to find knowledge and indulges in introspection, and prefers to be alone. It might be a temporary phase but a prominent one nonetheless. The person is looking internally for guidance as opposed to the outside world. However, it might cause the person to go into a state of withdrawal and remain lonesome. They might also be alone and spend time in isolation.

Wheel of Fortune

This card says that there is going to be a change in your life. It shows that your destiny and fate are about to change based on influences. The wheel of fortune signifies a significant change. It might be a change in fortunes or in life in general. The wheel of fortune is generally seen as a positive card that brings forth positive changes. It puts forth a change in destiny. However, on the negative side, this destiny might change for the worse. It can signify a negative change. The person's luck might go out of the window and a lot of bad luck might ensue. The person might not have a control over the forces that are controlling his or her destiny.

Hanged Man

This card says that you have given up or sacrificed a lot in life and that you might have to in the near future as well. It signifies the loss of something in your life that you have willfully sacrificed. You have let go of something important or there is a restriction on something you do. The negatives here include delaying something that is important to you. You have decided to be a martyr and you suffer from immense indecision. All of this is negatively impacting your living.

Death

This card does not necessarily imply impending doom. It could be that you have to change your habits. It just means that you will be moving on from a certain path of living into another. So it will probably be the death of one phase of your life and the beginning of another. Many people panic at the sight of this card but there is no need to worry, as it does not signify anything bad. However, it might mean that you are not allowing any change to come through and are bent on holding on to something that wants you to let go. You are not able to move on to bigger and better things in life.

Devil

This card shows that you are ignorant about the surrounding and the situation that you are in. it is all about sexuality and materialism. It is literally like the devil is seeing over you and exploiting your sexual nature to the highest limits. The reverse card tells you good things. This means that you will be detached from materialism and are leading a chaste life. It implies that you have broken the chains and are free of control. You have reclaimed your power and are now leading a good life.

Tower

This card shows that you will make a revelation about yourself very soon. It signifies a disaster that might come through or a sudden change or upheaval in your life. This can be in regard to your life in general or a certain aspect of it. The reverse of this card signifies the avoiding of dangers and the upheaval of fears. However, the person will be afraid of a change and not be open to it.

Star, Moon and Sun

These astronomical bodies depict the softness, brightness and enlightenment that are related to the moon, stars and the sun respectively.

The star signifies hope and also a positive outlook towards life. The card is meant to stand for prosperity and inspiration. It also deals with serenity and the need for calm. On the reverse, it stands for a lack of faith and deals in despair. It also has discouragement as an ill effect.

The moon signifies an illusion and possibly insecurity. It also deals with fear and a lack of confidence. On the reverse side, it signifies security and hope. There is a lot of confusion and unhappiness that is removed and dealt with. There is growth and positivity.

The sun signifies brightness and also deals with positivity and vitality. There is a lot of warmth and growth that is associated with this card. However, there is also a lack of success that can come about and might also lead to some temporary form of anxiety and stress.

World

This card depicts that you are contented and happy with yourself and the way your environment is. It signifies that you have successfully completed something and are facing travel prospects. The reverse of it signifies a lack of closure and also a sense of incomplete endeavors.

The Minor Arcana as opposed to the major Arcana indicate the driving force that operates our daily life. It depicts the concerns and the emotions that we endure in life. There are 56 cards divided into four suits, just like the cards – Wands, Cups, Swords and Pentacles.

Chapter 6: Spreads Or How To Position The Cards For A More Realistic Reading

Now that you have a basic knowledge of the main meanings of the cards, we can move on and learn about the way in which you can spread the cards for your readings. There are multiple ways in which you can do that, and many experienced readers develop, over time, their own ways to get to an answer for a specific question. However, the most important type of spread is the Celtic Cross. This is the most common, and, by learning its rules, you will be able to move to the other more complicated spreads.

The Celtic Cross

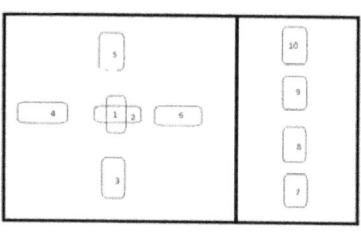

Elements:

The Circle. This section (the one with 6 cards) is representative for feminine characteristics. It is composed of two circles: the minor (the two cards from the middle) and the major (the two lines that surround the minor cross). The cards from the middle represent the most ardent worries at the moment of the reading, the cards from the horizontal line (from left to right) represent your evolution from past to present, and the cards from the vertical line (from the bottom to the top) represent the distinction between your unconscious and the conscious.

The Staff. This section (the vertical line of the four cards) is not necessarily related to the question, but it gives you a universal understanding of your position in life. It is also known as the "side comment" section.

Hence, there are 10 possible positions of the cards, and the following paragraphs will give you an insight on the ways in which you can interpret a certain card according to the position in the cross. I've drawn the numbers on each card, in order to make it easier for you to see what each position refers to.

Position 1. The card in Position 1 is the central concern of the matter (you or the problem concerning you). It represents your own position in the situation and it should tell you the main (dominant) quality that you should take into consideration.

Position 2. Just like it is situated (crossing the main problem), this card represents the additional element that influences your situation. This is usually unpredictable, and contrary to your main source of information. It may also represent what stops you from solving a certain issue.

Position 3. The traditional interpretation of the card in this position is "that which is beneath you". Thus this might be the unknown source of your problem, the element causing your major trouble. This usually lies in the unconscious, being the result of your hidden, rejected desires.

Position 4. Being in the position of the past, this card will show the element that is holding you back, and stopping you from living entirely in the future. It doesn't have to be something negative, but it's an issue that has been completed, and should not have the same importance in your present.

Position 5. This card will show what you consider, at the moment, to be the absolute truth (your present desires, preferences, or even worries). This is what your conscious projects as the most desired option for the future.

Position 6. A card in this position will tell you about the element that might become your focus of attention in the near future. It's either something that you have started a long time ago, and didn't bring complete, or something that needs to be taken care of right now.

Position 7. The card in this position will describe the way in which, even at the unconscious level, you perceive yourself and your own position in the world. This includes your personal abilities, your degree of self-confidence, your fears, limitations, and the ideal self.

Position 8. The elements of the card in this position represent the way in which others perceive you at the moment or, as the tradition says, "that which surrounds you". This might be a general impression of the world, about your way of being or others' opinion about the way in which you have dealt with a specific problem.

Position 9. This card will give you insight on the elements that you should have considered, but, for some reason, you refused to acknowledge their importance for the solution you are looking for. It can also represent your unconscious fear, and source of anxiety. In any case, this needs to be confronted as well, because it can represent a key to your problem.

Position 10. This card will give you a brief description of the outcome, the way in which things will settle down in the end. This can include the effect of your actions on other people, and on the entire environment surrounding you.

Chapter 7: Complete Comprehension Of The Minor Arcana

A tarot deck has a total of 78 cards. It has been established that 22 of these cards are within the Major Arcana, which leaves the balance 56 cards that make up the Minor Arcana. These 56 cards of the Minor Arcana are further divided into four distinct groups, with each group having a total of 4 cards in it. These groups are each aligned to one of the four elements, and each the groups are known as suits.

Within each suit there are ten cards that have been numbered from the ace until the number ten, and then there are four court cards, just like you would find in a typical deck of playing cards. The cards which have numbers offer a reflection on the situations that one may face in every day of their life, and the cards which are representative of the court reveal ones personality or are connected to people who are in the lives of the seeker.

The suits are explained as follows: -

The Suit of Cups

This suit is directly related to the element of water. Cards that appear in a spread from this suit will represent ones emotional state, what is happening within their relationships and the depths of their feelings. These feelings that are represented are beyond what one may feel for themselves. They also include the feelings that a person has in relation to other people.

When you see one of these cards, it is not looking to deal with your logical deductions in a situation, rather, it reveals what is really happening within your heart and the way that you normally react to specific scenarios.

However, when this card is revealed in the reverse, it points towards a lack of control of emotions, and a situation where your expectations have little basis in reality. It may mean that within you, there something that you are repressing that is stopping you from being able to express yourself and your emotions.

As these cards are similar to what you could find in an ordinary deck, they can also be represented by an ordinary deck for the purpose of completing a reading. They would be the Suit of Hearts in such a deck.

The Suit of Pentacles

This suit is directly related to the element of Earth. Earth normally indicates stability, though in this suit, the cards actually are focused in money and material possessions, as they reveal information on one's financial resources and what they physically own. All material things are covered by this particular suit, and these also include what is happening within ones business or career.

When it appears in the upright position during a reading, it looks at what is happening in the finances, work and health, and how you have altered or modified out outer surroundings to result in what you are experiencing in this areas of our lives. This in turn ties in with the way you feel about yourself.

Then, when this card appears in a reverse position, it points to some negative attributes including levels of greed where one places too much stock on material goods, and in not taking care of one's body and health. It could also reflect a situation where the finances are not being well managed, or a person works so hard that other areas of their live suffer as a result.

In a normal deck of playing cards, this suit would be represented by the Suit of Diamonds.

The Suit of Swords

This suit is directly related to the element of Air. This means that it is able to represent rational thinking, as well as ones actual thoughts and their level of intellect. It also ties in to the amount of power that a person may have. From this power, the cards in this suit can offer insight into the way one uses their own force, how much ambition they possess as well as their ability to handle conflicts. In handling conflicts, one may take action that has a constructive outcome, though in some cases, the outcome could be destructive instead.

This is a suit that looks at what is happening within the mind, so that it draws conclusions on once mental consciousness. Swords have more than one edge, so it is necessary to find a good balance, otherwise one may toy with good just as easily as they would with evil.

While this suit communicates all these positive attributes, should it appear to be reversed when presented, it reveals some very powerful negative attributes as well. These include hatred, and creating enemies. In a reading, one may also be able to identify anger, as well as complete lack of compassion towards a person or a situation. In the worst case, this card could also point out possible abuse of an individual, both mentally and verbally.

This is the most powerful of the four suits. From a typical deck of playing cards, the swords would be represented by the Suit of Spades.

The Suit of Wands

This suit is directly related to the element of Fire. This is the last of the four suits, and it represents the spirituality of an individual, as well as what gives them ideas and inspiration. It also reveals how a person's energy may flow. When these cards appear in a reading, they show that one has determination to pursue a particular goal, and the strength and ambition to make sure that they meet this goal. These cards will reveal what is happening within you at the core, as they tap into your consciousness on a spiritual level. Thus, your personality will be revealed from the suit of wands cards.

In a reading, they address the different things that keep one busy in the course of the day. This includes working or staying indoors. They look at the different ways that one may take action with their time and activities.

When these cards appear in reverse, they have negative meaning, pointing out a situation where one indulges in impulsive behaviour, or where there is no purpose in one's life. These cards could also reveal what happens to a person who has lost enthusiasm in life and this feels as though it has no meaning.

Should a person want to conduct a reading using the traditional deck of playing cards, this suit is represented by the Suit of Clubs.

Chapter 8: Amateur Tarot Card Readings

As a beginner Tarot student, your choice of Tarot card games is the key to a successful understanding of the messages that the cards offer. It is important to find a tarot package that fits your style and personality and makes you comfortable. Some decks like Minchiate Tarot have additional cards that are not best for beginners but are an exception. As a Tarot novice, you will always have to choose in terms of beautiful Tarot game full of symbolism, so the problem is less to find a great set of tarot cards and more choose only one.

Eclectic Tarot

This page is probably the most comprehensive directory of tarot decks available for free online. While some of the more modern decks might not be there, it's a great place to shop for Windows Tarot deck suitable for beginners. This site also has a lot of tips and tutorials on the Tarot and its history, and it is a great free resource for your Tarot related questions. With over 1200 tarot and Oracle decks reviewed, and more added every day, you'll have plenty of starter tarot packages to choose from.

Llewellyn Worldwide

Llewellyn is an international new age publisher and has a huge collection of tarot games, books, and individual decks with beautiful artwork. You can browse some of the cards in many decks, and even get a free Tarot reading using a selection of them, which can be great if you try to figure out whether you connect with the specific symbolism of a deck or not.

Beetle

Scarabeo is an Italian publisher of tarot cards and books, among other topics related to divination, and their modern website offers a look at their extensive collection of tarot cards. They have a whole collection dedicated to tarot sets, which include introductory books with the bridge. If you are in the Gothic style artwork, they have several modern bridges inspired by fantastic creatures, such as fairies, mermaids, and vampires.

Choosing A Tarot Game For Beginners

There are no strict rules on that Tarot Cards are better to know about tarot cards, but many people will recommend easier decks near to the original tarot decks, than more modern with non-traditional card names or extra cards. However, it is important to choose a package that suits your personality, and many tarot readers will buy only those packages that I personally find beautiful or somehow attract. Navigate until you find a bridge that forces you to buy and use it to take your first steps into the Tarot world.

Tarot Through the Ages

Tarot, pictures, we are more familiar with today, evolved from the genre, board games, played in the 15th century in Italy, and it became popular throughout Europe over the next four centuries.

To thoroughly explore the history of Tarot, you can read Michael Dummet's great book, " The Game of Tarot: From Ferrara to Salt Lake City "(Duckworth, 1980). Dummet, a highly esteemed British philosopher, is the author of many books on tarot cards. His Tarot scholarship is extensive and provides much of the research available at the beginning of the Tarot deck and its variations.

Tarot originally was fun in the classroom for leisure, those with time and money to spend on games. I am sure that at that time, the cards were handmade and illustrated by artists, and each set would vary with the artist's individual representation of the card images. Especially from the 15th up to the 18th century in Europe, variations of tarot games were very popular and enjoyed by people of little wealth and intellect, very similar to chess or bridge. The Tarot of 1700 was a total madness throughout the continent.

There are several decks of tarot cards that have come to represent a familiar iconography, each with its own history, interpretation, and devotees. 15th-century Italian bridge Visconti-Sforza is probably the oldest surviving bridge of this era, with original cards in the collections of several museums around the world. These beautiful artistic images are often reproduced.

And the 19th-century version from the south of France, known as the Tarot of Marseille, is a very popular deck in Europe.

In the US, The Rider-Waite-Smith Tarot deck is most often used today. It was conceived by the well-known Tarot authority A. email. Waite, and published in 1902 by Ryder Co., the simplified graphic style of this deck retains the historical symbolism of previous decks, but seems to be fresh and accessible to modern sensibilities.

Other tarot scholars are convinced that Tarot has its roots even earlier. They see relationships with the Kabbalah, or with ancient Egyptian hieroglyphs. Cards, for games or prophecies, were used in China centuries before they found their way to Europe in the 14th century, and it can be the original embodiment of the Tarot.

It is more likely that Tarot cards were brought to Europe through card games that were popular in the Old World Of Arabia. In France in the 18th Century, Antoine Court De Gebelin promoted the concept that Tarot cards came from mystical practices in ancient Egypt, which is described in his multi-volume work, Le Monde Primitif. Another Frenchman, Etteillla, is considered the first to recreate the tarot as a "divination" device. Basically, it is the first tarot reader. Reproductions of his book Thoth Tarot and other publications of Etteilla are still available today.

Tarot Reading turned out to be a new construction during the embrace of the Victorian age of spiritualism and occultism, laying the foundation for what would become the Tarot of the New Age School we know today.

There is an extensive scholarship and research on the history of tarot cards, either from online sources or in libraries, for those interested in exploring the topic. But for most of us, the story is not as convincing as the question of how Tarot makes sense in our lives.

Steps To Giving a Great Tarot Reading

Becoming a good Tarot reader requires much more than remembering the meaning of tarot cards and knowing tarot cards. Reading tarot requires practice, patience, and, most importantly, the willingness to trust your own intuition. If you are reading for yourself or someone else, there are some very useful procedures to ensure good reading.

1. Prepare a quiet environment

Believe it or not, the environment in which you run and read tarot cards can significantly affect the reading. Not only can the environment affect you as a tarot reader, but it can also have consequences for the person being read. When reading tarot cards, it is always important to postpone your personal problems and fears. Creating a comfortable space to help you stay focused and calm will help you stay objective and neutral while reading. Rituals like lighting candles or burning incense can also help you get in the mood.

2. Choose a meaningful map

When reading tarot cards, significant cards serve as a representation of the person being read or the situation asking. If you use the card-marking to represent the reading in person, most of the readers of Tarot cards tend to use the court cards either by associating the physical attributes of the researcher with one of the court cards or by a combination of their astrological sign to one of the court cards. If you choose and the Access Map has a specific situation, you can be creative as you like. Depending on the severity of the application, you can choose a map of the main arcane or smaller arcane. Major arcane cards tend to be used for major environmental issues, while less obscure cards tend to focus on everyday concerns.

Meaningful maps will also help you stay focused on the person you are reading. In many tarot cards, this means that the cards are located in the center. Help the tarot reader interpret and help him identify the key questions that lie around the interviewer.

3. Choosing the right course of Tarot

Tarot decks are the layout of cards arranged in a certain scheme. Each location of the map in the range has a specific meaning. When individual Tarot Cards are assembled for the spread of tarot cards, their meanings can be used to create a kind of story. The Tarot reader then interprets the cards according to their position and the relationships between them at the bow.

As a tarot reader, it is important to choose the spread of Tarot, which corresponds to the question asked. If the question is, for example, about love, then you probably want to enjoy the spread of love. In some cases, it is recommended to create your own spread of tarot cards. This can be especially useful when it comes to more than one topic.

4. Formulation of questions

The way the interviewer frames or asks a question before reading it can have a significant effect on the overall usefulness of reading. The more accurate the interviewer with his question, the more likely it is that reading tarot cards will solve their problem in a particular way. It is also useful to put an end to this question. Open questions can reveal hidden or overlooked questions that would otherwise have been overlooked. Open questions can also help the tarot reader discover the main problems or other influences that can affect the person reading them.

5. Mixing Boards

There are several approaches to mixing cards before tarot reading. This is usually the point where you have to actually read touch the card (although some tarot readers don't want anyone to manipulate their cards). If you decide to leave the investigator to manipulate the cards, you need to make sure that they are responsible, focusing on how to mix so that this energy can be transferred to the card. There are also several approaches to the "cutting" of paper, among the most popular are that the interviewer cuts the bridge three times with his left hand.

6. How do I know your tarot pack?

Before giving tarot reading, I always encourage people to give them time to really know the Tarot game that will work. This will help you not only to get acquainted with the cards, but also to deepen the understanding of their importance and mutual interconnection in the spread of tarot. Inevitably, those who receive and read tarot cards as they will, always take your relationship with their own cards. If you do not know the game with which you work, it is likely to come when reading tarot cards.

Things You Didn't Want to Know About Tarot

Do you love tarot cards because of its aura of mystery, esoteric history, or magical qualities? If you think that Tarot Cards are peculiar because of one of these reasons, you will not like what I have to say in this book.

I will look at the real history of Tarot, and my research on it has led me to conclusions that are different from what most of you have read online, and may be different from the one that wants you to believe are the facts behind Tarot.

I enjoy using tarot cards for over 25 years, and I love tarot symbology and tarot divination. Still, I don't like it when uninformed people create a romantic/mystical fantasy story for these cards.

I collected the first ten pieces of information that I think tarot readers need to know about the origins of Tarot. These data were collected by art historians, map collectors, and my research in museums and libraries.

Number 1

For those of you who like the idea that Tarot Cards are a magical or mystical instrument that has been handed down since the Egyptian or even the Atlantis era, I'm sorry, but there is absolutely no evidence of that. Not only is there no evidence, but when you look at the first known tarot cards and look at how they were born, there is not even a possibility of connection with Egypt or the mythical Atlantis. I hear you say, "But I've seen maps that have Egyptian drawings or symbols on them!" And you might have, but these are subsequent additions to the work of Tarot, and the images on which the Tarot is based on do not have Egyptian drawings or symbols.

The First Surviving Tarot Cards are hand-painted decks that were made in Italy, around the year 1441. They were made for the Court of Filippo Maria Visconti, Duke of Milan (from 1412 to 1447), and these cards are known as Visconti-Sforza Tarot. This name was given to them because it was the name of the families for which these cards were created. We know this because the heraldry of these families was included in the maps themselves. Representations of family members are also used in Maps.

Number 2

It has been claimed that today's ordinary playing cards are derived from tarot cards. The Joker is a representative of the card of the Madman of the major Arcans. Sorry, but ordinary playing cards developed much earlier and entered Europe from the Islamic world around 1375.

Number 3

The combinations of tarot cards, as we know them, are very different from the original ones. Tarot costumes derive from Islamic playing cards that were coins, cups, swords, and Polo sticks. The game of polo was very important in Islamic culture, but it was not known in Europe when the cards arrived, so the suit of Polo sticks became known as the suit of sticks or sticks. In Italy and Spain, playing cards preserved the costumes of batons, coins, cups, and swords.

Number 4

Tarot costumes, as we know them, have evolved from these Islamic playing cards, and various occultists over the years have changed the original costumes to make the Tarot more magical or mysterious. Sticks/sticks/slats were changed to chopsticks, and the costume of coins was changed to Pentacles.

Number 5

For many years, there was a theory that gypsies brought tarot cards to Europe, and this notion, unfortunately, became an accepted "fact" in the history of tarot cards. However, we know that the Gypsies arrived in Western Europe in 1417, but playing cards were known in Catalonia, a region of northeastern Spain, in 1370, so the cards arrived 47 years earlier than the Gypsies. And in historical documents, gypsies are called only palm readers; they are not talked about using cards for divination until 1891. And even then, the cards they refer to are standard playing cards, not Tarot Cards.

Number 6

Tarot cards were not intended as a means of hiding esoteric information from ignorant or invasive Nations. There are many references to tarot during the 15th century, and all refer to tarot as a game. It is never mentioned as having been used in any other form during this period. It was conceived as a game and no esoteric connection, nor divinatory properties, was attributed to it until several centuries later. The most likely reason for his invention was that the Duke of Milan (Filippo Maria Visconti) wanted a variation on the standard playing card set he had used. He asked his artist Bonifacio Bembo to create an extension of this game.

Number 7

The images of cards in modern Tarot Cards are similar in some respects to the original tarot cards created by Bembo, but there have been some changes. Over the years, images on maps have been modified by occultists to make them more magical or mysterious. A good example of these changes is the card known as the fool. Rather than being shown as a naive and confident soul who dragged through the countryside with his faithful dog, he was originally depicted in rags, looking quite miserable. He was considered the weakest of all in the physical field. It was the classic "village idiot." The charter called the High Priestess was known as the Popess. The heiress was once called the Pope. The Hermit was known as the hunchback or the father. The Hanged Man was the traitor, and the judgment was known as the Angel.

Number 8

The main Arcane maps are based on Christian principles, not on esoteric or magical knowledge. For the major Arcanes, the artist, Bembo, decided to use an allegory of religious teachings that could easily be displayed in a series of images. If you look at the sources of the XV and XVI centuries and some of the first bridges that list the elements in a sequence, you will see a separate model emerge. This model shows the physical kingdom as the lowest form of existence, and then shows the path of Christian spirituality leading to their God. The last map of the Greater Arcane is the map of the world, and one of the first authors on the subject described this last map, as "the world," which is God the father. The terms "major arcane" and "minor arcane" are relatively recent terminology. Paul Christian, an occultist of the 1800s, introduced these terms in the Tarot. Again, these terms were given to tarot cards to make it more magical and mysterious. The word Arcana means mysterious or secret, and by granting the cards these Latin titles, it was imbued with a mystical quality that was never wanted by the original designers of the game.

Number 9

Some occultists believe that there is a direct link between the 22 ways of the Cabal and the major Arcanes. Pico della Mirandola was responsible for introducing the Cabal to Western occultists. Still, he did so more than 40 years after the existence of the Tarot cards, so the tarot images were certainly not based on or related to this Hebrew alphabet and magic system. If the cabalists had invented tarot cards, the first cards had Hebrew letters on them; and they would not have used images such as death or the devil, or photos of women on them. Jewish Kabbalists did not like images of this nature, nor those of the human form, because they were forbidden by the first commandment which constituted "cut images." And on the contrary, tarot cards do not appear in any way in kabbalistic literature. Tarot cards do not descend from Jewish culture, and Jewish cabalists today do not recognize tarot cards as part of their beliefs.

Any meaning between the Tarot and the Cabal is the result of four main things;

1) the occultists conveniently hid some basic ideas about the Cabal to better fit their theory about a game between the two subjects. For example, papers such as the Pope and The Last Judgment are obviously Christian, not Jewish.

2) when designing a Tarot deck, occultists often implanted additional symbols inside the Tarot card images to satisfy the Cabal. For example, Levi introduced on the magician's table the signs of the "elementary" suit to prove that this card represented "First matter" - the elements are the basis from which all things were composed.

3) occultists often organized the order of cards to better fit their theories. The

Golden Dawn exchanged Justice and strength to conform to the Jewish letters and correspondents.

4) with archetypal images such as tarot cards, it is not too difficult to see an esoteric system as similar to another system.

In 1778 Court De Gébelin and Count de Mellet were the first to suggest a link between the Tarot and the Cabal, and this was collected and expanded by Lévi, an occultist with dubious research skills. But because of Levi's high reputation in the magical world of that era, the association between Tarot and Cabal was simply considered a fact from that moment on, without anyone worrying about whether he was right or not.

Number 10

Elementary associations with the four seeds are another subsequent invention of the occultists and are not part of the original concept of tarot cards. Eliphas Lévi gave to Tarot the associations that are still accepted in most Tarot books today: batons / wands = fire; coins / Pentacles = Earth; cups = water; Swords = air.

Conclusion: tarot evolution is an information puzzle with pieces from scattered directions, and is derived from many cultures and many minds.

When you think about tarot cards, I would like you to remember that there are two main types of tarot decks, and they are very far apart from each other. We have historical Tarot, which was simply designed as a card game, and now we have modern Tarot, which was derived from and evolved from historical Tarot. The first tarot cards do not have mystical or magical qualities associated with it. The historical Tarot was an invention of the 15th century and was based on the cultural and historical and religious expressions of its time-nothing more, nothing less.

Modern Tarot has esoteric and mystical associations, but only because it was placed there in recent centuries, not because it is related to some ancient source of secret knowledge. To write all this, I'm not trying to belittle the Tarot or its heritage. I'm just trying to add a rational voice to the irrational accounts that some people think of passing as the "story" of tarot cards.

Modern Tarot has become a powerful set of mystical images that can legitimately be seen as a spiritual journey. It is full of magical, esoteric symbols and archetypes, making it a playground for the imagination. That's great! This is an important part of the place of the Tarot in today's world. However, when people promote a fictional story simply to heighten a subject's mystique, it undermines the value of its true nature when the truth is finally revealed.

The true history of the evolution of the Tarot is just as interesting as the factories. The original version may not look as magical or mysterious as its counterpart, but it is still fascinating. When you see an article that tells about the "mysterious and dark" origins of tarot cards, please delve deeper; you will find that the author did not bother to do serious research on the subject.

Chapter 9: Suit Of Wands

The suit of wands is a representation of those who are intuitive and clear-headed. It's also a representation of those who are compassionate. The cards mostly related to employment complications and career issues. It can also relate to movement in our lives such as new beginnings blossoming. The suit is associated with the element of fire and the people who are associated with the suit are organized, logical, businesslike, and energetic.

The meanings for the cards are as follows.

Ace of Wands

Upright, the ace of wands stands for power, creation, inspiration, new beginnings, and great potential. Reversed, the card stands for someone who lacks motivation, is weighed down and has delayed completing goals.

Two of Wands

The two of wands upright stands for progress, future planning, decisions, and discovery. Reversed, the card stands for a fear of the unknown and a lack of planning.

Three of Wands

Upright, the three of wands stands for someone who will experience foresight, preparation, and expansion. Reversed, the card represents someone who is delayed, has a lack of foresight, and will experience obstacles in their long-term and short-term goals.

Four of Wands

Upright, the four of wands card stands for a celebration, harmony, home, marriage, and community. Reversed, the card stands for a breakdown in communication and a transition that may be unwelcome.

Five of Wands

Upright, the five of wands signifies someone who is a current competition with someone else or a disagreement. There might tension, strife, and conflict. Reversed, the card represents someone who wants to agree to disagree and avoid conflict. They are diverse.

Six of Wands

The six of wands upright stands for someone who would like public recognition, a victory, and progress. They are confident. Reversed, the card represents someone who is egotistical, has a lack of confidence, and is disrepute. They will experience a fall from grace.

Seven of Wands

The seven of wands upright represents someone who is in a challenge or competition and will have perseverance. Reversed, the card signifies someone who is going to give up because they're overwhelmed. They may also be over protective in relationships.

Eight of Wands

Upright, the eight of wands card represents action, speed, swift changes, movement, and air travel. Reversed, the wand signifies a delay, holding off, and frustrations.

Nine of Wands

The nine of wands upright signifies someone who has courage, persistence, and resilience, but they will experience a test of faith. Reversed, the card represents someone who is always on edge, paranoid, hesitant, and defensive.

Ten of Wands

Upright, the ten of wands card signifies someone who has a lot of stress, burdens, and responsibility. They are very hard at work and may have an achievement in the future. Reversed, the card signifies someone who is trying to avoid responsibility because they have taken on too much.

Page of Wands

The pages of wands upright signifies someone who is enthusiastic and wants to be a free spirit. They are always exploring and discovering. Reversed, the card stands for someone who is a pessimist and has a lack of direction. They will experience setbacks to their new ideas.

Knight of Wands

Upright, the knight of wands stands for someone who has a passion, energy, lust, adventure, action, and they're impulsive. Reversed, the card stands for someone who will experience delays. They're very hasty, scattered, and frustrated.

Queen of Wands

Upright, the queen of wands stands for someone who is warm, vibrant, and exuberant. They're a very determined soul. Reversed, the card symbolizes someone who is aggressive, violent, demanding, and shrinking.

King of Wands

The king of wands upright symbolizes someone who is a natural-born leader, an entrepreneur, and a visionary. They're very honorable. Reversed, the card stands for someone who is hasty, impulsive, ruthless, and has high expectations of those around them.

Chapter 10: Swords

Swords are another name for spades in the original playing deck and they also stand for the element of Air and their cards are about reason.

Ace of Swords - Upright: someone who will experience a win, raw ability, a break-through, and mental certainty. Reversed: someone without accuracy, who is perplexed and tumultuous.
Two of Swords - Upright: bad premonition of someone who will struggle with uncertainty,

a deadlock, a block of emotions, and options. Reversed: bewilderment and being overwhelmed with facts. Not a good card to draw no matter what.
Three of Swords - Upright: awful breakup, agony, regretful, despair, and giving someone the brush-off. Reversed: delivery from physical suffering, and absolution.
Four of Swords - Upright: resting, recovery, meditation, inactivity, and lack

of interest. Reversed: no advancement and agitation.

Five of Swords - Upright: stress, fighting, misfortune, deception, and being overthrown. Reversed: past grudges and someone who is open to modification.

Six of Swords - Upright: someone who is sorry and going through a change of status.

Reversed: someone who can't go forward because they have a lot of burdens.

Seven of Swords - Upright: someone who is dishonest and disloyal. Someone who is sly and wants to do something without another's knowledge. Reversed: someone who is getting clear of mental disputes.

Eight of Swords - Upright: secluded, barred, and confined. Reversed: willing to try new things and new views, and undergoing deliverance.

Nine of Swords - Upright: someone having bad dreams, is discouraged and despondent, or feeling nervous or hopelessness. Reversed: helpless, discouraged and afflicted.

Ten of Swords - Upright: someone feeling betrayed, beaten, abandoned, that they've lost and their relationship is over. Reversed: someone who is getting better but will worries that it won't go well and there will be an inescapable end.
Page of Swords - Upright: someone who is inquisitive, chatty, and full of life. Reversed: someone who talks a big game but doesn't actually do anything about it, make pacts that they can't carry out, and don't give much thought about what they are doing.
Knight of Swords - Upright: someone who is careless, believes very strongly about something and talks about it, informative and do before thinking. Reversed: willing to break the rules because don't have concern for them, and feels spread out and disorganized.
Queen of Swords - Upright: quick on their feet, have everything arranged, insightful, and love to be on their own. Reversed: someone who has too many emotions and is unfeeling.
King of Swords - Upright: someone who is

smart, has clout, is strong and wants accuracy. Reversed: someone who shows unkind behavior, is devious and cruel.

Chapter 11: What You Need To Know About Shuffling Tarot Cards

How many routes to Rome do you reckon exist? Well, let us say, legal and illegal ones all considered, there are just as many as any devious mind would wish to try out. And even when it is all legal, you still have many ways of getting to that ancient city. Likewise, there are a myriad ways you could shuffle your tarot cards. And while there are none you can deem illegal, there surely are some that will not give you what you would call helpful results. So you need to know how to shuffle your cards so that you do not just get psychological consolation that you have been told something you did not know, but you actually get something that reflects the reality in your life. The long and short of that rather long discourse? Simple: For best results, follow the basic tarot card shuffling principles, namely:

Let the shuffling be free of manipulation

Let your intuition guide you

These are two, apparently contradictory, but still reliable principles that will fetch you dependable results that are closest to what you need in terms of answers, solutions or direction.

Ensure you create a bond between you and the tarot cards in use

How does that happen? Murmur some magic words? No – all you need is your touch and attention. Your energy never ceases to flow and so when you focus on the cards you are shuffling, a kind of bond builds between your inner self and the tarot cards. It is like you are magically creating a bond between you and those cards. In another aspect, you are creating a bond of a psychological nature. And it is that bond which develops from your card handling all the way leading to the reading. And card handling includes that part of making the spread. The psychological bond even involves that feeling of ownership that you bear as you prepare the cards.

As you can see, therefore, your involvement is having a big impact on the outcome without you doing anything that can be deemed to be manipulation.

And how much is this that you are doing to make this great impact?

Deciding how to shuffle

Deciding how much time to take doing the shuffling

Making the choice of what cards to lay in the spread

Ascertain the shuffling is random by doing it cards upside down

In this process, the assumption is that you are basically no magician, so there is no way you can tell the illustrations on the cards when they are facing down. And so you are succeeding in establishing randomness in shuffling.

And how does a single deck serve different people?

Hey! Your deck of cards does not contain information tailored to you as as x, y or z. In fact, that same deck that is in use now is not affected in terms of its ability to help other querents. You just need to shuffle the deck afresh for each and every reading; with, obviously, the sitting querent having his or her last say in the shuffling as well as the spread. So, essentially, for every reading, it is the energies and influences of the sitting querent that are at work.

In any case, tarot card reading is not about specific closed solutions. Rather, what you stand to get from card reading are choices that are open and available to you. Then with those various choices you can consider your situation and see what choice fits the bill; the option that has all the likelihood of bringing positive improvement to your life.

Your tarot card reader is not, for instance, going to tell you that you are going to receive a scholarship to a particular college even when you have not applied for it. No — a card reader is not at all a fortune teller or a prophet of sorts. A tarot card reader is someone who needs your input as a matter of necessity to be able to tell the possibilities that you could face if you do not do something about your life; or those that exist if you take one of many closely related courses of action.

Chapter 12: Why Psychics Use Tarot Cards

First of all, what is a psychic? Psychics are people who claim that they have the ability to use extrasensory perception (ESP). They use this ability to discover information that are hidden under the normal senses. Large industries and networks exists where certain psychics provide their help and use their talents to be able to advice and council their clients. Not only that, but the word psychic is also an adjective to describe the said abilities. Psychics can also be performers like stage magicians that use certain techniques like prestidigitation, cold and hot reading.

Take note, a psychic and a medium can be differentiated because they are not the same thing. A medium is considered a psychic, but psychics are not really mediums. The difference? Mediums contact the dead or the spirits that were never incarnated. On the other hand, psychics can be associated to fortune telling.

Another thing that should be clarified is the fact that psychic abilities come from the person who channels the readings. Psychic tools merely help the psychics in conducting the readings. It's just a little help, there is nothing wrong with that. These little tools, like the tarot cards, also serve another purpose.

You see, a lot of psychics get nervous and anxious during these readings. When this happens, just like anybody else out there, there are more prone to making mistakes. The tools serves as a kind of distraction, it's what they put between themselves and the curious client. Quite a lot of them stare into the cards or mumble a few words about the energy of the universe in such. But in truth, they take it as an opportunity to look into space and really work their psychic skills without worry.

Remember what we stated, the tarot cards can act as the psychic's special tool or crutch along the reading. But they do not really rely on the tarot cards themselves for real psychic information. Once they rely too much on the cards, they will limit their psychic or medium abilities.

Why is their psychic abilities better than the fortune telling tools? Let's call out an example, imagine going to another country to do some business or study. Of course you will have a picture of your family on your phone or on a photograph lying somewhere. The picture represents your loved ones, the ones that are there for you all the time. But wouldn't it be better of you could just go home and be with them for real? That goes the same of the tools, psychics need to develop the real thing and not the representation.

Why tarot cards? Aren't there any other tools? Well, there are other tools that they consider to be dangerous because these tools get used as games or parlor tricks. The first and most common on their list is the Ouija board, next in line is the voodoo doll, lastly the spells. Psychics can consider the Ouija board as the worst one because a lot of teenager use it as a toy and do stuff out of curiosity. Plus Ouija boards are really easy to buy. Ouija boards are not evil tools, bad stuff happens because they are not used properly. The main problem about Ouija boards is that it can easily call out evil souls, demons or any malevolent ghosts. They can haunt you, hurt you and interfere greatly in your lives.

Voodoo dolls can be good or bad, it all depends on the person who's going to use it. You should intend to help others with this. There are times when we think that offerings helps with people complying with what we want. For example, you have a best friend with a lousy boyfriend that you don't like. You want your best friend to dump him and look for a job. The goal is admirably all in all, but maybe she sees something in him that you just can't.

Another form of Voodoo doll is called effigy or the use of someone's picture in order to lose a couple of pounds. Grab your own effigy (it should be thin and presentable) and place it inside the refrigerator. This way, whenever you feel like eating, you can think of the effigy and set it as you motivation in eating healthier.

Lastly, the spell is similar to the Voodoo doll, it all depends on the intention. The most common and known spell is the love spell, but there are hundreds of more to choose from. So are these spells considered black magic? No, because it can only be called black magic if you use it to control or harm others. But, if you are using a spell that offers healing or something to improve the life of another, then that's white magic. Take note that spells like these don't work all the time, it only works if the person you are offering it to, accepts. You might wonder "who would refuse an offer of healing?" There are a few reasons as to why, one is that dying person has gladly completed their journey and want to accept their heavenly rewards. Another is that person is paying for some karmic debt that they had in their past life.

Let's go back to love spells, it's kind of a white magic, but you use it to manipulate another person. The best you can get from it is something temporary, a temporary feeling of lust and desire. If this spell is casted too strongly, then get ready for a either a super jealous lover or a crazy stalker.

Chapter 13: Tips

To finish up this book I want to give you a few tips as well as a little bit more information that will be useful to you while you are learning how to read tarot cards.

You need to understand that there are no rules when it comes to reading tarot cards. As you are learning you are going to come across a lot of information and this information may seem contradictory but you really should not worry about it. The truth is that no one is going to be able to tell you exactly how you should read the cards, it is completely up to you as is the interpretation of the cards when they are laid out in a spread.

Try reading a card before you look it up. Look at the picture on the card and try to determine what the card mean. Most of the illustrations on the cards depict the cards meaning which makes it easier for you to remember their meanings, you will be surprised at how much you are able to understand about the card just by looking at it.

Make sure you understand what each of the suits in the deck stands for. The cups represent water, emotion and relationships, the sword represents the air your thoughts and communication, the pentacles represent the earth, your physical body and health and the wands represent fire, the spiritual aspects of your life.

Personalize the tarot card meanings. I have given you the basic meanings for the cards but if you really want to interpret these cards you need to make these meanings more personal. Meaning what do the cards speak to you, for example for me death means putting away with the old and change is coming but what does the death card speak to you?

It is important to remember that while you are learning how to read tarot cards that this is a very personal process, while one person my tell you that one card has a specific meaning another person may interpret that card differently. The same goes for the spreads and the cards within the spreads. While you may read a spread one way I may read it completely different. Don't forget to make your tarot readings as unique as you are.

Chapter 14: Why Do You Want To Learn How To Read Tarot Cards?

Before you begin to figure out how to peruse tarot cards, one of the most significant inquiries you can pose to yourself is, **"The reason why I will like to figure out how to peruse tarot cards?"**

The response to this inquiry is significant in light of the fact that it will decide your decision of tarot card deck and how your readings, both for yourself and for other individuals.

The explanations behind needing to figure out how to peruse tarot cards are as various as the individuals who get the cards. Maybe you need to increase a more profound comprehension of yourself with the goal that you can utilize this data for your very own development and advancement.

Possibly you need to comprehend other individuals and their inspirations and activities, or utilize the cards in a training situation to quickly get to the base of constraining convictions and squares to progress.

Maybe you might want to build up your clairvoyant capacities, so you can settle on better choices throughout everyday life and business with the endowment of prescience, instead of thinking back looking back!

It might be that you have had readings from other individuals, which have been exceptionally useful to you and you might want to build up your very own instinct and innovativeness to take care of issues and difficulties throughout your life.

Tarot cards can likewise be an incredible apparatus to investigate your otherworldliness in more detail, going from some essential reflection to some a lot further crucial life questions.

Or on the other hand perhaps you are intrigued by the authentic imagery of the tarot cards or the more otherworldly and elusive domains of the Occult.

It might be that you have an energy for a specific time ever, or a specific culture or belief system or folklore or possibly that you are captivated by an individual and their work and those variables can likewise influence your decision of tarot card deck.

Your decision of deck likewise relies upon your experience as a tarot card per user and how far you have built up your clairvoyant capacities since certain decks are simpler to work with as a novice and some are progressively fit to increasingly instinctive readings.

When you know the motivation behind why you might want to figure out how to peruse tarot cards, at that point it is a lot simpler to pick a tarot deck that you can without much of a stretch work with. You would then be able to stay away from a great deal of cost and disappointment of picking something that you can't work with.

Rundown the Reasons why you need to figure out how to Read Tarot Cards

What stops you or has halted you in the past from Learning to Read Tarot Cards?

All reasons are substantial. It is essential to see what has prevented you from Learning to Read Tarot Cards before. This may have been an absence of time or sentiments of overpower or perplexity or you didn't generally like or continue ahead with the tarot card deck you have been working with or you attempted to learn in a manner that didn't generally suit you, for instance, you attempted to gain from a book, though you may have better tuning in to a seminar on an audio.

It may likewise be because of profound established convictions about the tarot and what it is or isn't or emotions that you don't have the mystic capacities you may require so as to have the option to peruse tarot cards for yourself or others.

Regardless of whether any of those things are valid or not, is really superfluous. The way that you trust them and any of them have prevented you from already learning tarot, makes them significant.

Rundown every one of the reasons that have halted you Learning to Read Tarot Cards or caused you not to complete a course of study?

Do you have a particular consuming issue or would you say you are searching for a general perusing or simply inquisitive?

Is it accurate to say that you are hoping to affirm your instinctive emotions about an issue?

It is safe to say that you are attempting to contact a friend or family member in soul? Assuming this is the case, you will most likely need to address a medium and attempt some otherworldly and psychic preparing.

It is safe to say that you are hoping to control yourself, and simply need a little help to explain your reasoning?

It is safe to say that you are searching for something to offer you decisions and a substitute future dependent on YOU settling on various choices?

Is it true that you are searching for something to give you some expectation and confidence so you can push ahead?

What would you like to have the option to do when you have done the perusing? Would you like to feel enabled to make some move?

Feel just as squares to progress have lifted and you can push ahead?

Settle on a significant choice?

When you know your very own inspirations for looking for figuring out how to peruse tarot cards you can set that as a basic expectation.

"I need to figure out how to peruse tarot cards in light of the fact that... .

I am searching for somebody who can push me to...

If it's not too much trouble control me to perfect individual for me, for the most elevated great of all concerned"

Trust your instinct to direct you to correct individual. The more clear you are on what kind of perusing you need and the sort of individual you need to manage, the simpler it is to draw in the best individual to support you.

You may end up on a specific site or get a desire to call somebody you have known about or frequently a proposal will come up in a discussion about something different.

Watch for those instinctive prompts and follow up on them.

Chapter 15: Second Septenary:
Arcana 7 To 12 Androgony

7TH HEBREW LETTER (ZAIN)

ROOT OF THE SYMBOLISM OF THE SEVENTH CARD OF THE TAROT

Hieroglyphically the Zain speaks to a bolt, and subsequently, it proposes the possibility of a weapon, of the instrument which man uses to administer and vanquish and to achieve his article. The Zain communicates triumph in every one of the universes. As a basic letter, it relates to the astronomic sign of the Twins in the Zodiac.

SEVENTH CARD OF THE TAROT

(THE CHARIOT)

The imagery of this card relates to all focuses on the thoughts which it communicates. A Conqueror, delegated with a coronet, whereupon rise three pushing Pentagrams of gold, propels in a cubical chariot, surmounted by a purplish blue, star-decked shelter bolstered by four sections. This image replicates the first and 21st arcana in another request for thoughts. The four segments speak to the four creatures of the 2 first Arcanum and the four images of the first Arcanum, images of the quaternary in afflicting its usual meanings.

The Conqueror, who involves the Center of the four components is the man who has vanquished and coordinated the rudimentary powers. This triumph is affirmed by the cubical type of the chariot, and by the Pentagrams which crown the Initiate. The Conqueror has three right edges upon his cuirass, also, he bears upon his shoulders the Urira and Tliummirn of the sovereign cleric, spoke to by the two sickles of the moon on the privilege and left.

In his grasp is a staff surmounted by a globe, a square, and a triangle. Upon the square, which shapes the front of the chariot, we see the Indian lingam, surmounted by the flying circle of Egypt.

TO SPINX

One white, the other dark—are saddled to the chariot. This Symbol speaks to the sacred septenary in all its signs. The word Yod-lie-vau-he is depicted upon the front of the chariot by the winged globe, to demonstrate that the septenary gives the way in-to the entirety Tarot. The two sphinxes compare to the two standards, dynamic and inactive. The Conqueror compares particularly with the Sword and with the Vau of the Sacred Name.

The entry from 011e world to the next is barely performed before we see a similar law in real life that we found in the first septenary. The second term of this arrangement will be the impression of the main, j Rundown as the second term of the primary arrangement likewise mirrored the first. Hoverer, since this second septenary is the focal one, we will discover, as the establishment of all its constituent arcana, the possibility of intercession or harmony.

8TH HEBREW LETTER (HETH)

Hieroglyphically the Heth communicates a field. From it springs the possibility of anything that requires work, inconvenience, and an exertion. Proceeded with exertion brings about the foundation of harmony, between the pulverization of crafted by man achieved by Nature, when left to herself, and the conservation of this work. Subsequently the possibility of adjusting force, and therefore of Justice, credit to this letter. 1

1 This letter, a go-between in (He) and 3 (Kaph), the one assigning life, outright presence, the other the family member

life, absorbed presence, is the indication of rudimentary presence: it is the picture of a sort of harmony, and appends itself to thoughts of exertion, of work and of ordinary and administrative activity.

THE EIGHTH CARD OF THE TAROT

(JUSTICE)

The thoughts communicated by this Symbol are of Equilibrium in the entirety of its structures. A lady has seen with a full face, and wearing an iron coronet, is situated upon a position of authority. She is put between the two sections of the sanctuary. The sun-powered cross is followed upon her bosom. Here we discover the continuation of the symbolical of the second and fifth arcana.

The situated lady involves the Focus between the sections, offering a first thought of the balance among Good and Evil. She holds a sword, point upwards, in her correct hand, furthermore, an equalization in her left.

Mysterious science (2), from the start hypothetical, has become pragmatic (5) and has been educated verbally. Presently it shows up in trouble the savagery of outcomes, horrible for the bogus Magi (the Sword), however just toward the genuine Initiates (Balance). The meaning of this Arcanum is focal between the fifth (n He) and the eleventh (3 Kapli) arcana.

This card is the supplement of the eleventh, as the fifth was of the second. In the first septenary afflict the cards which, by expansion, framed the number 7, finished one another; in the second septenary afflict the cards which, included, structure 1.9, act similarly. The eighth card of the Tarot speaks to the origination in the safeguarding of the subsequent card. It combines in itself the significance of the second and of the fifth card of the Tarot and speaks to the reflex of the seventh.

The basic presence is the methods by which the astral vivifying liquid or astral light (7) shows itself through the ether or astral issue (9). This is exhibited by the accompanying Arcanum.

9ᵀᴴ HEBREW LETTER (TETH)

ROOT OF THE SYMBOLISM OF THE NINTH CARD OF THE TAROT

(THE HERMIT)

Hieroglyphically the Teth speaks to a rooftop and proposes the possibility of a position of security, assurance. AU the thoughts emerging from this letter are gotten from the collusion of security and assurance guaranteed by astuteness. Cosmically the Teth compares with the zodiacal indication of the Lion. An elderly person strolling, bolstered by a stick. He conveys prior to him, a lit light, and half-covered up by the incredible mantle which envelopes him.

This image is halfway between the 6th and the twelfth. Insurance is demonstrated by the mantle which envelopes the elderly person. Intelligence is recommended by the half-concealed light. The stick shows that the Sage is constantly outfitted to battle against Injustice or Error. By contrasting this card and two others, the 6th furthermore, the twelfth, we will see that the clean-shaven youthful man in the previous (sixth) has picked the correct way.

Experience won in the work of life, has rendered him a reasonable elderly person, and reasonability joined to shrewdness will securely lead him to a more significant level, which he is on edge to accomplish (twelfth card). The bolt shot by the virtuoso in the 6th Arcanum has become his help, and the brilliant aureole which encompassed the virtuoso is presently detained in the light which controls the Initiate. This is the consequence of his delayed endeavors.

The ninth card of the Tarot speaks to the third, considered as preserver and beneficiary. It additionally balances the seventh and the eighth. Humankind satisfying the capacity of God the Holy Soul.

THE HUMAN CREATIVE POWER

The astral liquid, in this way, speaks to the general safeguarding of the dynamic powers in Nature. Here closes the primary ternary of the septenary of Preservation. We will currently observe the impressions of every one of these terms in the following ternary.

10TH HEBREW LETTER (YOD)

ROOT OF THE SYMBOLISM OF THE TENTH CARD OF THE TAROT

The hieroglyphic importance of the Yod is the finger of Rean; the pointer reached out as an indication of predominant. This letter has, subsequently, become the picture of potential indication, of profound term, and, in conclusion, of the unending length of time, with every one of the thoughts identifying with it. See the investigation of the word Yod-he-vau-he. The Yod is a basic letter; cosmically it relates to the zodiacal indication of the Virgin.

TENTH CARD OF THE TAROT

(THE WHEEL OF FORTUNE)

Two head thoughts are communicated by this Symbol.

1. Command, of Supremacy.

2. The possibility of a span, of the interminable activity of the time.

The wheel of fortune suspended upon its hub. To the correct Anubis, the virtuoso of good rising; to the left Typhon, the virtuoso of malevolence plummeting; the Sphinx is adjusted upon the Center of the wheel, holding a sword in its lion hooks. The principal thought is communicated by the ternary, Anubis or positive, Typhon or negative, the reasonable Sphinx, the ruler. The subsequent thought is communicated by the wheel, a line without a start or end, the image of forever.

The tenth Arcanum is halfway between the seventh and thirteenth arcana. 7 + 13 = 20 20=10. It communicates the relentless balance which adjusts the Creative acknowledge of the septenary by the important pulverization through Death

(Arcanum 13). The three arcana, 7, 10, 13, relate precisely with the Hindu trinity or Trimurti. It speaks to the course of things as indicated by the ternary law, which coordinates every one of the indications.

The tenth card of the Tarot initiates the negative part of the second septenary and communicates the thought of the septenary considered in its appearance. Without a doubt, the Creative power has changed progressively in the widespread vivifying Fluid (4), and the astral Light (7); presently it is spoken to by power potential in its indication.

We will see this mightily showed in the following Arcanum.

11TH HEBREW LETTER (KEPH)

ROOT OF THE SYMBOLISM OF THE ELEVENTH CARD OF THE TAROT

The hieroglyphic significance of the Kaph is the hand of man, half-shut and in the demonstration of demand, similar to the Gimel. Be that as it may, the Kaph is a fortification of the Gimel, so that we may state that it assigns the hand of man in the demonstration of getting a handle on emphatically. Thoughts of solidarity are along these lines applied to this letter. The number 11, the first after the decade, gives a diverse incentive to the Kaph, which assigns a responded, temporary life, a sort of shape, which gets also, reestablishes each assortment of structure.

It is gotten from the letter Heth, n (8), which is itself got from the indication of supreme life, Heth, n (5). In this manner, partnered on one side to the indication of rudimentary life (see the eighth Arcanum), it joins to the connotation of the letter Heth (n) that of the natural sign j (Gimel) (third Arcanum), of which too it is just a support. The Kaph is a twofold letter, comparing cosmically with March and Tuesday. The quality, effectively potential in its indications, has demonstrated its full power in the eleventh Arcanum; it will balance itself in the accompanying Arcanum.

THE ELEVENTH CARD OF THE TAROT

(STRENTH)

Just two thoughts are communicated by this Arcanum 1. The possibility of solidarity. 2. The possibility of imperativeness. A little youngster tranquility shuts a lion's mouth without any noticeable exertion. First thought, this little youngster wears the imperative sign coupon her head.

Second thought, the eleventh Arcanum is halfway between the fifth and fourteenth arcana. In it, we discover the imagery of the eighth Arcanum moved to the physical plane. It is, in reality, a picture of the power given by the sacred science (second Arcanum) when evenhandedly applied (8).

12TH HEBREW LETTER (LAMED)

ROOT OF THE SYMBOLISM OF THE TWELFTH CARD OF THE TAROT

Hieroglyphically the Lamed assigns the arm, and hence it is associated with whatever stretches, that raises, that unfurls like the arm and has become the indication of broad development. It is applied to afflict thoughts of expansion, of occupation, of ownership. As the last sign, it is the picture of the power that got from the rise. Divine extension in humankind is created by the prophets and disclosure and this motivates the possibility of the uncovered law.

Be that as it may, the disclosure of the law includes discipline for him who disregards it, or rise for him who gets it and here we discover the thoughts of discipline, of rough passing, deliberate or automatic. The Lamed, a basic letter, cosmically relates with the zodiacal indication of the Balance.

TWELFTH CARD OF THE TAROT

THE HANGED MAN

A man hangs by one foot to a gibbet, settling upon two trees, each bearing six branches, which have been cut off. The man's hands are bound behind his back, and the overlap of his arms shapes the base of a turned around triangle, of which his head is the peak. His eyes are open and his reasonable hair skims upon the breeze. His correct leg crosses his left thus frames across.

This youngster is again the Juggler whose changes Ave has just followed in the first, sixth and seventh arcana. Like the sunset amidst the indications of the Zodiac (six on each side, the trimmed branches), our youthful saint is again suspended between two choices, from which will spring, no longer his physical future, as in the sixth Arcanum, however his profound future. The twelfth Arcanum fills the Center between the sixth Arcanum (Wisdom) and the fifteenth (Fatality).

These arcana speak to the two ladies of the sixth Arcanum, respected in the profound sense. This Hanged Man fills in for instance to the pre rich, and his position shows discipline, the total accommodation which the human owes to the Divine. Considered catalytically, the

Hanged Man shows the indication of character.

In the Hermetic evaluation of Rose Croix (eighteenth degree of the Ancient and Accepted Rite), one of the indications of acknowledgment comprises crossing the legs like those of the Hanged Man. It is obvious that the starting point, what's more, the significance of this sign is very obscure to Freemasons. The twelfth card of the Tarot speaks to Equilibrated Power. It kills the restrictions of the tenth and eleventh cards.

Adjusting power is the last term of the second septenary. By it the Astral will acknowledge itself, to go into the physical, from the universe of conservation and gathering (second septenary) into the universe of change (third septenary).

Conclusion

Tarot reading is incredibly exciting. Even if it might appear challenging to you at first, you can definitely become a pro at reading Tarot cards with some practice.

Thank you again for purchasing this book!

I hope you have learned how to read Tarot cards and are excited to get started.

The next step is to get yourself a deck of Tarot cards if you don't already have one and start practicing reading the cards.

Thank you and good luck!

www.ingramcontent.com/pod-product-compliance
Lightning Source LLC
Chambersburg PA
CBHW071450070526
44578CB00001B/289